AUTHOR UNIVERSITY

7 Steps to Writing & Self-Publishing a Book

By

Greg Justice, MA and

Kelli O'Brien Corasanti, MS

Contents

INTRODUCTION

When people dream of writing a book and getting published, they normally dream of a big publishing house picking up their book and distributing it all across the country in every bookstore that exists. That's a huge dream and it has happened before. But, it doesn't happen as often as you might think.

After looking at the statistics, let's be generous and say that 250,000 books get published a year. That is only a small portion of the million or more books which are written in a year. The publishing house 'gatekeepers' go through all the books that are submitted and they make a small pile of the ones they like. They might send letters out to the authors they reject, but sometimes they don't even bother to let an author know. Those rejections are tough. When you have poured your time, energy and emotion into your book, it is really hard to be told it won't be published, or worse yet, to feel ignored or dismissed by not even hearing anything from the publisher.

The fear of those rejections keeps so many people from even writing a book. Others take the leap, write the book, but then never risk sending it out to be published for fear that it isn't good enough. And there are countless others who have been rejected and simply give up after that. That happens to so many authors, and it's a sad conclusion to a perfectly good dream, especially when there are other options available. One option, in particular, is self-publishing.

Self-publishing used to have a negative connotation, but not anymore. It is being taken more and more seriously because great books have been released in the self-publishing category. When the gatekeepers of the publishing companies let really great books slip by, those authors look for other options. Self-publishing is a great option!

If a person is determined, self-publishing is an excellent solution to getting your book out there in the public eye for people to enjoy. You can even live the life of the bestselling authors if you are willing to do most of the work yourself. Set up book signing tours. Get radio station and television show appearances. Yes, you can do all these things if you have the drive and the hustle to make it happen.

Ironically, self-publishing used to be the way it was done. Many classics that are revered today were self-published by their authors at printing houses. The printing house would do a run of possibly a few thousand to start, and then the author handled the business of selling them. That practice became less common when publishing companies started to form because there were huge profits to be made. Publishing companies would swoop in and give writers deals they could not refuse. Who would turn down an advance while the publishing company offered to handle everything from distribution to promotion?

Although self-publishing was the original way things were done, authors just got out of the practice of doing business that way. The great thing is, however, that self-publishing is back and it's bigger than ever. With the power of the internet, authors are proving they can do it themselves and some are making small fortunes with their work. The fact of the matter is that self-publishing is now out-pacing traditional publishing. Hachette, HarperCollins, Macmillan, Penguin Random House, and Simon & Schuster, otherwise known as the Big Five Publishing Companies, only account for 16% of all books sold on Amazon. Self-published authors are taking significant market shares in all genres and they are particularly dominating sci-fi/fantasy, mystery/thriller, and romance genres.

In the category of E-books, self-publishing accounted for 31% of all sales. In addition, independent authors (also known as 'indie authors') account for 40% of all E-book revenue. Indies are normally priced higher and they are raking it in.

It is also important to note that 25% of Amazon's bestseller lists are self-published books. Self-published books have placed number one in their categories and have made it to the New York Times Best Seller's List as well as Oprah Winfrey's Book Club. Where $.99 used to be the sweet spot for E-book sales, $2.99 to $3.99 is common now. The old model is out the window and the new self-published model has taken over.

As you're reading this, you might be asking yourself what it takes to make a self-published book that successful. It's a great question! The reality is that not all self-published books will get there and some self-published books aren't even worth the paper they are written on. To be successful, you have to distinguish yours from those. You need to care enough to perfect your work and make the time to do it. You have to learn about self-publishing and you have to discover the tools that will make it work.

Self-publishing has once again established itself as a legitimate way to get a book in the market. It's a multi-million dollar a year business. If you pay attention to the trends and learn what works, then anyone who wants to write a book can make a splash in the publishing industry today.

Does that sound intriguing to you? Are you ready to take your idea and write a book? Are you excited to find ways to get your book out into the marketplace so you can share your knowledge, ideas and experience with others? If so, then you're in the right place.

This book will teach you every step you need to take in order to put a top notch book together. It will also show you how to get it out in the market and sell it. We have compiled this step by step system based on our years of experience in self-publishing and our knowledge of writing and marketing. Together we will show you how to make your dream of becoming an author a reality!

Ready to begin? Then let's get started!

CHAPTER 1

What is the purpose of your book?

If you're reading this book, you have a reason for writing your own. What your purpose is for writing a book will dictate how you proceed. You could be into writing for the love of it or you could be trying to inform readers of something very important.

To establish themselves as experts, doctors, real estate agents, carpenters, and coaches have all written books to teach their readers something about their trade. Having a book puts professionals on a whole new level of professionalism. A carpenter can start in his field of building houses and parlay that into being a guest on television shows because he wrote a book about his trade.

A doctor can easily move from wiping noses in a children's clinic to being a medical analyst for a top notch news channel because he published a book about medicine. Anyone in any field can benefit from writing a book. The rewards are endless and it's an exciting journey when you finally get on it.

Writing for the love of it or writing to become the expert are only a few reasons for writing a book. There are entrepreneurs who only want to write a book to get rich and it's a great way to make that happen. You just have to be smart. You can't just throw words on a page and think everyone's going to buy it. Just the opposite, you can't write the world's greatest novel and not put any marketing into it. A good book doesn't just sell itself and that's something so many other authors fail to wrap their brains around.

It's good to properly identify the purpose you have for writing a book. That way, you can map out how you are going to write your book and then market it. The fundamentals are the same. Only a few things change from book to book.

Writing for Passion

When you write a book because you are passionate about writing, it's writing of a whole different kind. You can either make up the story as you go or outline it beforehand so that you know exactly how it's going to end. You get to discover it along the way.

You can write it as a narrative as if you are telling the story to someone who is sitting in front of you. You can write a comedy, a drama, or a fantasy. You have so many choices when it comes to just writing with passion. Just start from the beginning and bring the story to life.

When you are finished, the editing process has several purposes. One of the main things writers do wrong when they are writing a story from their own imagination is they leave gaps that have to be overcome. Gaps in a story leave plenty of questions.

If a reader has questions, a good writer will make sure the book has the answers. A gap in the story will leave a detail wide open and that makes the whole novel fall apart. It takes a good eye to look for those and that's why even the most professional writers need good editors. It's not just an amateur move. It happens to the best of them.

But having passion to write doesn't always mean writing fiction stories. Having passion to write means you can write anything. You might want to inform people about something that is important to you. Write a book about a political or a social issue. Write a book about hunting and fishing. Write a book about the environment and natural disasters.

You can write a book to inspire others. Maybe you've been through something that most people can't imagine. If they can't relate, they want to know how you made it through your struggle or got out of your situation and are where you are today.

Sometimes your audience though, they will be able to relate. People who have gone down the same roads as you and who have met with the same challenges, they'll read your book too because it might help them with their situation. You might become their hero they follow for encouragement. They don't have to know you. They just like to know they are not alone.

While you may be inspiring others in their walk of life, you are also accomplishing something else. Having a passion to write a book also helps with your personal growth. It is the art of discovery that helps people solidify what they know about themselves. It's like a personal behavioral exercise, only on a much larger scale.

You certainly can learn more about yourself through your writing. The phenomenal trick is that you don't have to write about yourself to learn more about yourself. Personal discovery and personal growth can happen in anything that you are writing. How do you feel about the social issues? How do you feel about the natural environment? No matter what you are writing about, not only are you informing readers, but you are informing yourself.

There are so many books to be written. That's the best thing about wanting to write a book and having passion about it. There is no end to subjects and there will never be an end to readers. They are biting at the bits for the next book to get their hands on and you can be in the right place at the right time to make it yours.

Writing to Build a Platform

A person might have a whole different purpose for writing a book. If they are passionate about the ice melting because of global warming or if they want to do something about the oil spills and all the wildlife that was affected, a book is a great way to get their message out to the many readers they can reach.

That's called building a platform. A person can build a platform for a variety of reason. Of course when people talk about a platform, most listeners immediately think about politics. A book can certainly help a candidate get elected into office. In fact, it has many times before.

Just like a doctor or a coach establishing themselves as gurus in their field by publishing a book, a candidate can establish himself as a knowledgeable person in the many issues they'll face in office. Not to name any names, but quite a few candidates have written down their thoughts on subjects and gotten them published. That's how a person raises their relevance in the eyes of the media and in the public domain.

For some reason, a book lends more credibility to the author. When you compare two candidates, be honest and think about who you would vote for in the election. The candidate with the book seems to be more credible than the candidate who hasn't written one. It's a great strategy to employ in any situation. But, it definitely works great in politics.

Certainly, politics isn't the only reason a person would want to build a platform. However, it does play into that same kind of strategy. If a person is interested in creating change, maybe they want to create awareness about animal abuse or shady adoption agency practices, writing a book is a great way to not only get the message out, but to put the author in front of a camera where he can discuss the issue in greater detail.

Stretch your creativity and imagination to figure out how you can best use building a platform as a purpose for writing a book. Write about financial strategies in today's economy. Write about cost effective ways to feed the homeless. Write about whales in captivity and build your platform. Get the whole world listening to you.

Growing Your List

A great online strategy for building a business is to grow a list of names and emails. Not so that you can sell them and annoy everyone who has ever trusted you. But so that you can email your list and keep them informed, keep them interested, keep them active, and to keep them coming back to your site time and time again for different deals you have to offer.

In order to build a quality, responsive list is to get them interested in something that has value in the first place. That's what attracts them to you. They want to read what you have to say.

Fitness training is the type of field where this strategy is perfect. If readers are interested in different exercise techniques, a book is a great way to get them to sign up to the list. You can offer your book for free if they sign up. These are motivated email users. Your list will be packed with active addresses who will respond to future emails because they trust what you're sending them.

If the book was informative on certain exercises, how to strengthen muscles after an injury or how to begin an effective weight loss program, the readers are motivated. Future emails could be about other related strategies or products that might interest them. A growing list is a great way to start an online business and a book can be used very effectively to get one up and running.

Writing to Make Money

Of course, the idea of writing to make money is nothing new. That is the dream for many writers. Entrepreneurs and opportunists capitalize on it all the time.

While there are some writers who only love to write as an art, in the back of their mind is the idea that they can make a lot of money and sit on top of the world with the bestsellers. The problem is that it doesn't always happen. That's what has some writers very discouraged about the decisions they've made in life.

The truth is that there is money to be made. That's why people are still writing books, still selling them, and then going back to the drawing board to do it all over again. So if something works, why be discouraged about failures in the past? Just learn from those mistakes and move forward. There is money to be made out there for everyone. It's time for you to get in there and carve out your piece of it.

There is no shortage of readers and there is no shortage of subjects that they will buy. Ironically, some of the most successful money making books on the market are from financial advisors teaching readers how to make money. Other great books are in the DIY category. If you can teach anyone anything, write a book. People will buy it.

CHAPTER 2

Creating a Mind Map

Once you've identified the purpose for writing your book, you are ten steps ahead of everyone else who just starts writing. That's because you can't just start writing words on a page and think that you'll have a book in no time. Narratives are even tougher to write when you start that way.

You have to pour your thoughts out about the subject. Even if it is a narrative, writing down everything you know about your characters, your setting, and your plot will help you know where to begin. But, that's for a narrative.

The purpose of pouring your mind out onto paper is more for the informative book, the book that teaches readers something or makes them aware of certain issues. No matter what your subject is, you have to organize your thoughts in some way. You have to get them out of your brain and somehow in front of you so that you can see them. Then, you can work with them.

There are plenty of strategies for doing that. Not every strategy is for everyone. You should learn them all and then choose the one that makes you more comfortable and more productive.

Different types of Brain Dumping

Brain dumping is the act of getting everything in your mind out and stored in some way so that you could retrieve it later. That's more or less a technical way of saying to write it all down or to create a file in a folder on your computer.

Some people prefer to grab a pen or pencil and go to town in a notebook. It definitely works. But staring at a blank piece of paper can seem daunting for a beginner. How many times were you determined to write something? But when you got out the pen and piece of paper, the thoughts suddenly stopped coming?

It's called writer's block and there is a great way to get out of that. When you sit down in front of the piece of paper, try this simple exercise. It works every time.

Freewriting Exercise

Some people try it for two minutes. Some people go for ten. But, start with the first thought that comes to mind. Don't worry about what you are trying to write about. Write the first thought that comes to mind no matter what it is. Then keep going with each thought that comes in your head.

Examples: I think I might have left the coffee pot on. My car needs a tune up. I can't remember the last book I read. But, it was something about a guy trying to find another guy. Wish I could remember what that book was about...

And it continues. Those thoughts have nothing to do with what your book is going to be about. But, they are going to break your thoughts free. That's the strategy. If you keep going for a predetermined amount of time, you will eventually start writing thoughts and sentences that do have something to do with what your book is about. Those are the beginning thoughts that will help you organize.

The rules for freewriting are that there are no rules. Don't worry about spelling or grammar. Don't correct your mistakes. Just write for that predetermined amount of time and keep writing until it's over. When you read back through what you wrote, you'll find your thoughts and that will help you get started.

Typing

If you are more comfortable with typing, by all means start there. You can also do freewriting this way. You just change the mode from writing with a pen to typing for a set amount of time. Everything else stays the same.

When you type, it actually puts you a few steps ahead. You don't have to take what you've put on paper and transcribe it. You can simply store it in your file. Retrieve it any time you want. Work with it. Make changes. You're making the writing process a whole lot easier for yourself.

Talking into a recording device

If you have trouble with either of those writing methods, you can record your thoughts with a recording device. Most people have them on their phones these days. Simply talk into it when you have ideas and then save the files.

You can transcribe your own thoughts later. Type them down and put them into a file. Or you can have someone else do it. Transcription is certainly not a lost occupation.

Some people have stepped up their game though. There is great software out there that can take someone's recordings and transcribe them into text files. Good software needs to be taught a few things about the person's voice and the words he uses, but then the software takes it from there with fairly good accuracy.

Dragon NaturallySpeaking is probably the best transcription software out there. You can speak into it or you can record your voice and let it transcribe later. The accuracy gets better the more it knows your voice and the words you use. The software might be a little pricey, but it pays for itself if this is something you're going to be doing more than once.

Mind Maps

Once you have your thoughts out of your brain and dumped into a file of some sort, a mind map is a great way to organize. It might look like clutter to others. One person's mind map is another person's chaos. That's okay. As long as it makes sense to you.

A mind map is done best when there is plenty of space to work with. Some people use index cards to write down different thoughts. Other people simply take it to a chalkboard or whiteboard.

Place the central theme in the center of a bulletin board or write it in the center of a whiteboard. Then, you can map out subtopics from there. The fact that you have space to build makes it easier to keep going into smaller and smaller sections as you get further away from the main theme.

For instance, a main theme of a book could be Achieving Success. A subtopic would be about setting goals. That goes into personal goals as well as setting work goals, career goals, and education goals. Distinguishing work goals from career goals, what you do now as opposed to what you will be doing in the future for the long haul.

Now, you're three levels deep into your mind map and you can keep going. Each area of goals would need something more specific. That's a mind map. That's why you need a lot of space to fit everything into it.

Of course, there is also software that can help you make a mind map. MindView is great Mind Mapping software that helps you organize your thoughts in many different ways. Pick the mode that best suits you and your diagrams come in handy throughout the rest of the writing process.

CHAPTER 3

Creating an Outline from the Mind Map

You've been working at your mind map for days. You have put it down and walked away from it. You've come back and moved things around. When you step back, you're finally at peace with it. What do you do with it now?

The ideas and the thoughts are all there. You've put in the work. Now, it's time to take the mind map and use it to outline your book. Some people have said they thought mind mapping would take up a lot of time. But, it actually saved them time.

They were able to take what was on the mind map and create an outline with their thoughts. The General Theme is the main reason you are writing the book. In an outline, it would most likely be the name of the outline or it would be the introduction. When you write a book that is meant to inform, a good introduction into the main theme is a great way to start.

Your subtopics are the numbered, bigger ideas of your outline. They are probably the chapters of your book or they could quite possibly be huge sections of the book with a few chapters in each. It depends on your book's organization.

If you are writing about finance, investing might be an entire section of your book with several chapters dividing up everything that investing is about. That's how huge a book can get if it is organized that way. To keep it simple though, you might want to make your subtopics into a chapters. Then, you can break everything else down accordingly.

The mind map helps you stay organized. Under each chapter are the more in-depth details of that subtopic. In an outline if you have numbers for subtopics, then the more in-depth details are represented by letters.

Example:

1. A Book on Finance

    a. Introduction to Finance

    b. Why is it important?

    c. What you need to get started?

2. Investing

    a. Knowing the market

     b. Getting started

     c. Having a strategy

     d. Building a portfolio

3. Saving

     a. Creating a savings plan

     b. Following through

     c. Keeping your savings safe

4. Retirement

     a. Planning ahead

     b. Downsizing

     c. Keeping track

In that impromptu outline created above, the main theme is that it's a book on finance. The subtopics are indicated by numbers as Introduction to Finance, Investing, Saving, and Retirement. Details that go into further depth on the subtopics are indicated by letters.

Outlines are pretty easy to construct once you get the hang of where the information goes. The mind map you have created at this point helps you understand how to put the outline together. When the outline is in place, all that's necessary at the point is to follow through. Start writing!

But before you do that, there is something you might want to know. The Mind Mapping software that was mentioned earlier can help tremendously at this point. You might want to stick with putting index cards on a bulletin board or writing everything out onto a whiteboard. If that's what makes you comfortable, then by all means do it your way.

The Mind Mapping software though helps to map everything out from the brain dump you've been working on all along. Once you have created your mind map, you can put it into outline form simply by the push of a button. That saves a tremendous amount of time and it takes guessing out of it.

You can start with a general theme and start adding subtopics. When you realize that a subtopic isn't right, you can simply move it where it fits into the mind map better. Create as many topics as you want. Create as many subtopics as you need. Move them around and get them organized the way you want. Software does tend to take the pain out of doing things.

Then, put it in outline form. That's what you've been trying to do all along and mind mapping software has just streamlined the process. Look into it. As mentioned before, MindView is good. But, there are several others to fit your comfort zone and budget. It can get you ten steps ahead of where you would be if you can abandon the old dinosaur ways of doing things.

CHAPTER 4

Writing Your Book

You may have been jumping up and down, screaming about when do you actually get to start writing your book. You've thought about the purpose. You have determined what the book is about and you've mapped it out. When do you start actually writing it?

That time is now. Start going through your outline and adding in the fine details that make your book unique. If it's about fitness, what do you know about fitness that you want the world to know? If it's about building an online business, start filling in the details and letting people know how that works.

The thing is at this point, you might finally realize that not everyone is a writer. You might want a book. You might actually need one. But, you might not know how to write one. Not everyone has the ability to sit down and pour all their thoughts out into a book.

Of course, there are always naysayers who would come along and wonder why you would want a book if you can't write one. They don't make a valid point and don't let those kinds of thoughts keep you from moving forward. The thing about it is that not everyone's a writer. But, everyone has something they can write a book about.

If you have done all the work up to now, you've mapped out your book and written your outline, there's a lot you can do at this point to finish your book. You have options. Of course, gutting through it and doing it yourself is the first option. Everything in your life, you've had to at least try first before you got better at it. Writing could be one of them.

Obviously, another option is that you can hire someone to write it for you. You can hire someone to do anything for you. Of course, there's a perfectly good ghostwriter who can take your words and put them into a book for you. But, let's try something first.

Let's Try It On Your Own

If you are going to try writing the book yourself, the one thing that hinders most people is how to get started. Ironically, you already know how. When you get asked a question, do you wonder how to begin answering it?

Normally, people already have answers. They don't even hesitate. Writing can be the same way. Just ask yourself a question. How you answer your own question is how you should start writing your book.

If you were talking about pitching a baseball and you had ten kids in front of you who were trying to learn, do you think you'd find it hard to teach those kids how to pitch? If you were a baseball coach or a baseball player, chances are you could talk about pitching for days and never lose one person's interest.

That's how you have to handle writing. Write about it like you talk about it. Remember when you were freestyle writing and you didn't care about punctuation or grammar? Treat this part of the writing process the same way. Just start writing like you're explaining it to your audience.

Use the same informal language you would use if you were standing in front of them. Act like you're giving a speech if that helps. But, get the information to flow out of you just like the brain dump exercise. Only this isn't bits of information that make up an outline. This is huge chunks of it that are going to make up your book.

Writing Schedule

You can develop a writing schedule that pushes you through the task of writing an entire book. When do you have time to write?

When you sit down and actually write, how much can you write in an hour?

Do the math and the next thing you know, you have a schedule that outlines how much you are going to do per day and how long it's going to take you to finish. If you don't deviate from that plan, you'll have your book in that timeframe. It's that simple.

With the outline, you'll know what you need to write next. With the subtopics and the greater details in the outline, you'll never get lost. Just sit down at the time you have on your schedule and begin writing just like you're teaching a room full of people.

Make sure you discipline yourself. This task is just like any other you've accomplished throughout your life. Studying when you went to college. Working on projects at work. Raising kids. Getting better at your career. Getting better at your game. There are so many things that you can motivate yourself to do when you want to do it. Make writing your book one of them.

Transcription

Like I mentioned earlier, transcription is not an occupation that has gone away. It's just a little different now. You can send your files to a virtual assistant and pay about a dollar a minute. Some can offer a turn-around as soon as a day. If you have about two hours of recording, that comes to just over a hundred dollars and your draft is ready to go.

It's that easy. So if you have a problem writing your words down or typing them on your laptop, get used to speaking into an app on your phone and recording your voice. You can write book after book that way if you just get into the habit of recording your thoughts when they hit you.

Of course, I did mention transcription software. This is a good task for it. It can handle small work. But, good software can also handle huge recordings and type them out for you with pretty good accuracy. The accuracy is based on your voice and how much you teach your software. It picks up on your vernacular and gets better as it goes.

Be willing to spend some money on good transcription software if you choose to go that route. Of course as mentioned earlier, Dragon NaturallySpeaking is probably the best software out there for transcription. They say you get what you pay for and this is one of those items where it's absolutely true. Cheap software will turn your recordings into a bunch of jumbled letters and numbers. The better software is a little bit more expensive. But if this is something you are getting into, you will be using your software over and over and it will eventually pay for itself.

Freelance Writers

Welcome to the world of freelance writers. There are many out there and they are waiting for you to ask. Freelance writers are ready to take your thoughts and create a book out of them. It's a fairly simple process based on your comfort level.

There are sites where you can submit a job description. If you've done your research, you'll find several legitimate sites you can trust because they have ways of filtering out weak writers and letting the cream rise to the top.

Guru.com and Elance.com are probably the best among all of them. They have qualified writers who build portfolios and get rated according to their work. They also get tested and qualified. When you submit a job description, you'll be able to easily pick the more qualified writers from the bunch and narrow down your list.

Once you've created a job description, you'll get plenty of bids. So, get ready to screen. Contact a few writers. Ask for writing samples. Narrow down your search to a short list. Pick the one you want and go.

The freelance writer obviously wants all the notes and files he can use. But even if you don't have much, you'll find a freelance writer who can take everything you have and turn it into something. Good ones offer research and sometimes, they are already familiar with the topic. You can stipulate these criteria in your job description and you'll find the freelance writer you need.

Anything you know is worth sharing. Any idea you have is worth following through. An architect doesn't build the building. He puts the plan together and builders build it. Whether or not you can write your own book makes no difference. You have something important to say and if you have to hire someone to write it for you, at least you are moving forward with your great idea.

CHAPTER 5

Editing Your Book

Regardless of how you got your book written, whether you did it yourself, had it transcribed, or found a ghostwriter to do it for you, it's going to need edited. This is the part of the process that takes your draft and turns it into a polished piece of work.

That's why it's not all that important to make sure you dot every "i" and cross every "t". You can allow some of your thoughts to be out of order. You can show up with a stack of papers or you can have it all in a folder in different files like a total mess. This is where you get your hands dirty and start putting it together the right way.

In the writing process, there is prewriting that you have already done and then there is writing, which you have just completed. The next steps are rewriting and then editing. Some people think of these as two different steps whereas some people think of them as one. It doesn't matter as long as you get them both done.

When it's broken down, rewriting is content editing. Editing is copy editing. That's what those terms would actually stand for in the publishing process. What's the difference between content editing and copy editing?

Content Editing

In a narrative, there are characters and settings, plot twists and story arcs. In content editing, you are making sure that all the details are in sync. Can a character change? Yes, but it has to be explained by the story. Can you have a plot twist? Yes, but it has to make sense.

Content editing is going back through your story and making sure that the details are cohesive. For instance, the characters are consistent and they are believable. If a character comes from Boston, he sounds like he comes from Boston. You might not be able to hear him through the written word, but a good writer can bring it out in him. That's what content editing is.

In content editing, you're looking over the plot of the story and you're making sure that all the twists have purpose, that they

34

are believable, and that they leave no gaps. That's why you might have to rewrite part of your story, so that you can fix all those errors.

Of course, that's content editing when you are talking about a drama or a sci-fi, a work of fiction you wrote to tell a story. How does content editing work in a nonfiction piece about global warming? It's still very critical.

Content editing is also about fact checking. You want to make sure that the things you say are factual. Also, you want to make sure that any calculations you might have made are right. Fact checking is everything down to a simple sentence. If it's not worded right, it can mean a whole different thing. A content editor would pick up on that and make sure the sentence says exactly what it was meant to say.

Copy Editing

Every book needs copy editing. When we talked about content editing for different types of books, it was made clear that task would be different based on the nature of the book. But, copy editing is the same no matter what book it is.

When you are copy editing, look for grammar mistakes as well as spelling mistakes. Most of the time, writing software can be relied upon to be right in picking out errors. But, not all the time.

Spelling errors occur when you use the wrong word in a sentence. To, too, and two all sound alike. They are called homonyms. But, they don't mean the same thing. It's very important that you use the right word in a sentence otherwise you end up with a very gross error like, "I went two the store."

It throws a reader off and downgrades the credibility of the book. If you don't think so, you'll be very surprised. People think about these things. If you didn't take the time to make sure you used the right word in a sentence, what else didn't you take the time to do? That's a very legitimate argument and that's why editing is so important.

Hire an editor

It might cost some money, but it's worth it. It could mean the difference between a reader putting your book down because it has spelling mistakes and him telling all his friends about it.

There are freelance editors who can look through your book and put those final polishing strokes on it. If you get the right one, he knows what he's looking for because he's done it a thousand times. He can have your book turned around in no time and ready to get published.

The process is the same as hiring a freelance writer. You can even go to the same site and put in a different job description. When the proposals come flying in, narrow down your search, and go for the best qualified editor you can afford. It's worth it to pay the extra money for a good editor than to hire a poor one for less money and end up with the same mistakes you had before.

Editing really does mean the difference between a great book and one that's mediocre. Think of it as your last set of eyes before it goes out to see the world. That is because it is. The final editing of your book should be given a great amount of care and even possibly done more than once to make sure you are putting your best product forward.

CHAPTER 6

Self-Publishing

Now is the time that you have been waiting for. You are about to see your book through as you envisioned from the start. The process from here can even seem long. But, every step is worth it.

When you are self-publishing, how long this process takes is pretty much up to you. You have to make some decisions along the way and then you can set your work free and watch it perform while you do everything you can to insure its success.

Is your book going to be an e-book or a paperback? Of course, it can be both. But, formatting is different for both. Being aware of that going in makes all the difference in the world.

When you are publishing a paperback, the company you are publishing through will send you a template. It's not hard to figure out what to do. But, some people like to leave this part of the process in the hands of a professional.

You can find one through the same channels where you found your writer and editor. But if you want to try it yourself, the template isn't that hard to follow. You'll have a book cover template based on the size of the book you specify. You can allow the cover art of the book cover to run all the way out to the edge. But the title, the author's name, and the description all need to fall inside the border called the bleed area.

Book Cover

When you self-publish through reputable online self-publishing companies, they offer book cover suggestions. You can use their work if you want. Sometimes, it doesn't cost anything to choose from the selection they have.

But, here are some tricks you might want to try. Of course, you can take a photo yourself and make that your book cover. Whatever inspires you or comes to mind when you think of your book, capture that image. A book about nature could have trees on it. A book about medicine could have a picture of a hospital on it. Nothing's stopping you from taking the photo yourself.

If you don't want to take the picture, you can Google the image. The same thing applies. If you need a picture of nature,

Google search "nature" and see what pops up. But, adjust your Google settings so that you can use any image you find on the cover of your book.

It's not hard. Simply, Google "nature" or whatever your term may be. When your search is complete, click on "Images" at the top of the search so that it shows a wide selection of images relating to your search term. When images come up, click "Search Tools." A new line will show under where you'll see "Usage Rights." When you click on the arrow, either "Labeled for reuse" or "Labeled for reuse with modifications" will narrow your search to images that you can freely use for your book cover without worrying about anyone contacting you over copyright issues.

Now, all you have to do is learn how to use image software. This book is about writing and publishing a book. Not about a whole other category concerned with imagine manipulation. But if you are tech savvy in any way, GIMP is great software that you can get for free and it is comparable to Photoshop. Download the software and create your book cover.

If that's over your head, then you just might be better off using the free images and templates the self-publishing company has available for you. Either that, or you can hire someone to do it for you. There is a site online called Fiverr.com and you might be able to find someone artistic enough on that site to create a book cover for you for exactly $5.

The interior of the book will have a template too. But if you can read specifications, you can adjust your manuscript in your word-processing software. Basically, the margins are what you need to focus on. Inside margins change based on the page count. Outside margins normally stay the same. The header and footer also have some specifications you'll need to adjust or they won't pass the initial review.

An e-book on the other hand, has an entirely different set of criteria. Chapters should be linked on the table and the chapters should link back to the table so that going back and forth is made possible. Fonts have to be readable by every device. Images should be centered and not aligned with text. Plus, images need to be compressed to a certain size. That just scratches the surface. There is quite a bit you need to know.

If you've ever looked at a book on a device, then you know it doesn't look the same as the printed copy. The fact that the device has to display it different is the very reason why it has to be formatted correctly.

You can read up on it on a dozen websites that teach you. You can also put your manuscript through one of the many conversion sites that are available. But, you might want to stop and think about what you're doing first.

There are a few self-publishing sites online that are very trustworthy. They are valuable in the sense that they have the ability to get your book placed in Amazon and all over the net.

Plus, they streamline the process of self-publishing every step of the way.

Why make the process harder than it has to be? Go with the company that already knows everything about online publishing. They've been doing it for years.

Createspace

Amazon is the biggest book selling website online. They sell every book imaginable. If it's out there, if it's being sold online, you can find it on Amazon. So, why don't you leave your publishing needs in their hands too?

Createspace is the self-publishing company that works hand in hand with Amazon. They help you every step of the way and make it as easy as possible. Simply have your manuscript ready when you go through the process because it's so quick from the time you start to type in your title to the time you actually have to upload your manuscript.

You will be given a legitimate ISBN and your paperback will be available all over the net. It will obviously be listed in Amazon where you can search it every day and show your friends. But, it will soon start showing up across the net in places like Barnes & Noble, Alibris, and Ingram just to name a few. It happens automatically, but it takes a while.

Your listing shows up on Amazon first. Then, it filters to the rest over time. Amazon is motivated to allow other online book sellers to sell your book. They still get proceeds for those sales. So, it's a great service to go with for every step along the way.

As an added perk, they can easily format your book into an e-book for distribution with their other company Kindle. KDP, better known as Kindle Direct Publishing, is another amazon company. That's how you get your book to be available through Kindle devices Amazon sells. What a hookup?

It's an easy process that it walks you through. There are some things you might have to adjust once you start going in that direction. Don't worry! It will let you know what's going on every step of the way. Once it's ready to be distributed through Kindle, you'll know and the sales will start to grow if you do your diligence and follow through.

At that point, claim your author page on Amazon so that you can write what you want in it and introduce yourself to the world. When you search for your book, you'll see that it's available in print and in kindle. Plus, you'll see that your name now has a link. That link takes you to the author page where if you have more than one book on Amazon, they are all listed there.

It's a very streamlined process that leads to the most success because it's hooked up to the biggest online book selling company in the world. The thing is though, it's not the only way to get things done. In fact, Amazon offers exclusive package deals that might sweeten the deal a little bit. It's just that, some people aren't interested in being exclusive.

Lulu

If you'd like to get acquainted with the company that pretty much started it all, Lulu is one of the original Publish On Demand companies that made it easy for users to publish their own books. Not many other POD options were available in 2002 when Lulu was established.

Between Createspace and Lulu, there aren't that many differences. Lulu will offer you a template for the cover and the manuscript so that you can adjust your settings and get it right according to their publication guidelines. They will make your book available in online booksellers like Amazon, Barnes & Noble, and Ingram.

They offer an e-book submission tool that allows you to turn your document into a epub or PDF. They have a creator guide to help you properly format your manuscript and make it e-book ready. Of course, they also offer experts to do it for you. If you have the money, it's always a good idea to pay someone who knows what they're doing if you are not technical savvy and can't figure it out on your own.

So, there is very little difference between Createspace and Lulu. You'd just have to look through everything they each have available and figure out which one fits what you need. For one thing, Lulu offers screenplay coverage as well as treatment and screenplay preparation.

That means that you can either touch your toe in the water and see if your manuscript could be made into a movie or you can have it written into a script and go all the way. The choice is yours. But, the price does go up depending on what you want. If you think that's the direction you'd like to take with your manuscript, by all means let a professional writer turn it into a screenplay and submit it to a legitimate talent management company that will take it into consideration.

Yes, they actually have a management company that will look at your screenplay. If they like it, they will contact you and you can either become talent they manage or enter into a screenplay deal with their production company. It gets a little too real at that point. But be ready, if that's what you want.

Lightning Source

Lightning Source is Ingram Book Company's print on demand vendor. There are plenty of differences between Createspace and Lightning Source. But, the main difference really is if you plan on starting your own publishing company.

That means, you want to publish plenty of books. You are going to purchase ISBNs for your books and give your publishing company a name. Of course, you can start with one book. But when you compare Lightning Source to Createspace, you'll realize why Lightning Source is more for the independent publishing company than for the independent author.

Smashwords

If you just want to put your book out in e-book format, Smashwords is a place you can go. They have a submission process that takes the manuscript and produces it in many formats including Epub, PDF, and Mobi in addition to a slew of other formats some people would consider obsolete.

But, let someone with an old device or a different device come along wanting your book. Smashwords will have the right format just for them. They will have a PDB for the old palm readers and an LRF that only Sony readers can read.

Smashwords does drive traffic to its site where your book could be visible to thousands of viewers. But, it doesn't beat the visibility of Amazon. And if you go into an exclusive deal with Amazon, which could benefit your sales, you wouldn't be able to have your book available on Smashwords.

CHAPTER 7

Marketing

This is a very critical stage in the whole process of publishing your book. If you have done everything right up to this point, this is where it can fall through. Marketing is what gets your book in front of people so they can make a decision to buy it.

But, it's tricky. The internet does make it easy. It's just that some people start off the wrong way trying to market their book and they never get anywhere. One of the most common mistakes is trying to market your book to other people who are trying to market their book. It's a bunch of people selling to each other, but no one's listening.

It's actually called spamming. It's just that some people let you get away with it and some online groups actually encourage it. Some Facebook groups let you go on their page and post an update status about your book. The thing is, that's actually a waste of time. Everyone there is trying to sell their book. You're just another on the pile no one is going to even see.

Speaking of spam, it's not effective at all. It will get you nowhere. So, let's go into a few strategies people use to spam so that you know what not to do.

Spam

If you join an influential group on Facebook and the first thing you post on their page is something about your book, you just spammed that entire group. Could you have sold books in that group? Yes. Are you going to sell books in that group after spamming them? No.

Spam comes in many shapes and forms. That's one of them. Spammers go on sites and sign up just so that they can post their advertisements. They have no interest in contributing to the conversation or being a positive part of the group. They either ended up getting booted and blocked or they get ignored based on the group's moderator.

Spam is also the practice of obtaining email addresses and then sending out emails advertising your book. Of course, it is legal to obtain email addresses. But, it's how you do it that makes the practice shady.

Some people put their emails on their social media profiles. Sometimes, emails can be obtained by looking them up in databases or email address collection sites. The rule of thumb is that you can obtain a person's email legally if they opt-in to your list. If you scrape the internet for email addresses, that's the wrong way.

Emailing people who want emails from you is the right way of doing things. These are the people who might have gone on your website and signed up for updates. But emailing people who have no idea who you are and aren't expecting an email from you, that's the wrong way. That's called spam and it's not effective at all. A person deletes those emails as soon as they see them, that is if they don't take it up on themselves to report your email address. So, it's a waste of time to even get into that practice.

Now that we've talked about the wrong way of doing things, let's talk about the other way...

Effective Marketing Techniques

First of all, you have to think way ahead of the game. When it comes to marketing, it's best to get started when you are several months out from publishing. There are things that need done before your book is available. It's best if you know what those things are because they can mean the difference between a successful book marketing campaign and a flop.

Getting Reviews

New York Times is a great place to get a review. But, you can't send them a book after it's published and expect to get a review. They like to know beforehand. They're not going to give every book they receive a review. But, it's not a bad idea to give it a try.

Run a few copies off for reviews. You'll be sending these copies out to reviewers before your book is actually published. Copies of your books that are run before the first standard edition run are called galleys. When you see a book reviewer ask for copies of galleys, that's what you want to send.

There are several strategies that help you get reviews. You can send them out to big publications that don't charge for reviews and see what happens. They'll want several galleys 3 to 4 months in advance and there is no guarantee you'll get a review.

Big publications include *New York Times*, Barnes & Noble, and the *Wall Street Journal* just to name a few. Perform a Google search and be willing to spend some time looking for perfect big house publications that have book review policies. Follow their guidelines and hope for the best. You may not get reviews from the big guys. But, you should always try and when you do get a review, that will make your sales fly right out of the gate.

Some book review sites offer good book reviews that come with their packages. You might have to pay for reviews. That's why you should always do your research and look at the company itself. While they're busy reviewing books, you should be busy reviewing them and see if they are even worth the time.

When you are researching reviewers, look at what they offer. If they have a good following on Facebook and Twitter as well as a healthy newsletter broadcast, they just might be a company worth paying to get a review. If your review stands a chance of being seen by a couple hundred thousand people in social media and in emails, then it's worth a shot.

You can also research all the reviewing sites online that don't ask for payment. If they have a decent following on Facebook and Twitter, they're worth looking into. Also, most of them request a copy of the e-book. That's an ideal way to go because it has no overhead. You can send out thousands of e-books to reviewers and build a nice compilations of reviews across the net.

Amazon and Goodreads are other places where book reviews are pretty important. But, those are unsolicited. Of course, there are ways to circumvent the system. There always is. You can look for reviewers who have reviewed other books and offer to send them an e-book to see if they'll review yours. You can send out copies to your friends and ask them to review your book. These practices are not frowned upon and the more you hustle, the more interest you'll get in your book.

Time The Release Of Your Title

A great strategy is to watch the news or what's going on in the world around you and release your title based on something huge you can link it to. Some people think this is a very difficult step to take. But, you'd be surprised.

If you are very creative, you can generate some great buzz for your book if you have it release at the same time something else is going on. If it relates, if it is relatable in any way, it's the perfect newsworthy story or even to link your book to. Once you being to understand the mentality you have to have for marketing, you'll see how easy it is to find the perfect newsworthy event.

Also, you can keep using stories in the media to promote your book. Every time something in the news happens that is any way relatable to your book, use it to your advantage. Write an article and publish it on your site. Share it on Facebook and Twitter. Get the buzz going again. Don't ever let it die. You can always find a way to make your book relevant.

Write a Press Release

Some people get confused about what a press release actually is. They think they can just write a press release up about their book and then submit it everywhere. Actually, that's the worst idea. That's not an effective press release and it will get your book nowhere.

An effective press release is newsworthy. What makes a press release about a book newsworthy? It depends on the book. But something can be pulled out of every book that makes it worth printing in the news, whether online or in print.

In one particular case, a book was written that mirrored an actual event. But, the book was written before the event took place. The press release covered how the event was practically predicted and that's what gave the book another push in the media.

How you write a press release is simple, but it takes some practice because it's not a sales pitch and that's what most people get in the habit of writing. When you write a press release, start with a dynamic headline like you are a reporter.

What is it about your book that makes it newsworthy? Answer that in one sentence or less and you have yourself a headline. Then, write your body. Remember, you are writing like a reporter.

Answer who, what, when, where, and why. Then, provide contact information so that anyone in the news can get in contact with you. Always, put a quote in the press release. Some news agencies won't even call you to pick up your story. They'll just use your quote and write their article. It's good to provide enough information in the press release in case that happens.

You can submit to several different online press release distribution companies like PRWeb and eReleases, which uses

PRNewswire. But, you'll also want to look up editor information on specific publications and send out your press release to them personally. Local newspapers want your story. Send a PR to every single one of them and the local television channels while you're at it.

For local news, sometimes a good PR is just about the fact that you're a local author. If you come from a small city, they'll eat that story up and possibly even put you on the local news channel for an interview. That's a good way to get some material to use for further online advertising strategies.

The larger publications and news channels want newsworthy stuff. Their idea of what's newsworthy is very different. So, it's a bit harder to come up with something that will make them bite. Just don't think it's not worth it. Put your press release together like a journalist and send it to them.

List Your Book On Other Sites

There is a plethora of sites out there and some are hard to get onto. But, there is a trick to it. People aren't interested in you until you give them something to get interested about. If you build your online presence and people start to notice you, now you're interesting to them.

Start by submitting your book to several free sites. A great list to start with includes Addicted to e-books, Author Marketing Club, Books on The Knob, Digital Book Today, eBooks Habit,

EReader News Today, Free Kindle Books & Tips, Free e-books Daily, GalleyCat Facebook Page, Goodkindles, Meet Our Authors Forum, Pixel of Ink, Every Writer Resource. But, don't stop there. You should be getting the feel for what you can do if you perform Google search and get active with your online book marketing campaign.

Website

Building a website is very important to conducting a successful online campaign. It should be what you are about. At the very least, it should be what your book is about. But, your book can be used in so many ways to establish your online presence.

First, your website should have a very dynamic homepage. It should be clear and concise about what it is. It has to pop and get people's attention. It also has to be very functional.

Your homepage can sell your book with dynamic advertising and a sense of urgency. "Get it now!" "Don't let time run out!" "Only a few copies left at this price!"

In the sidebar, give people a way to sign up for further updates from you. Give them a reason. People don't want to just give their emails away because they are tired of hundreds of emails that they have to delete every day. Give them a reason to want to read yours. Offering an online course gives visitors a reason to open your email. Tips and tricks always seem to work if they are interested in what you have to say.

Your site should also have an About You page. Give them the information your visitors need to know that qualifies you as a person they want to hear. It doesn't have to be a long essay about your life. It can simply be a review of your accomplishments and what you are about. That's good enough to get your readers interested in reading your book.

Of course, your website should have a page about your book. The advertisements are all over the site in headers, footers, and sidebars. But, an entire page goes into greater depth. It can simply be the description that you have on the back cover. If that's what's selling your book, that's perfect for your book page.

Have a way to buy the book on your site. You don't need a checkout or a shopping cart. A link to your Amazon page is actually more effective. They would be more willing to go to Amazon to buy your page than to submit their credit card through a site they don't know if they can trust.

Look around at other websites. Get a feel for how they look and how they do things. Then, get to work on your own. You can have a website up and running in five minutes. These days, they are not that hard.

Go to a domain register like Godaddy.com where they sell domains and they have hosting packages. Purchase your domain and hosting package that fits your needs. Once you are into your account with your hosting package, have Godaddy install Wordpress on your domain and you are ready to roll in 5 minutes.

The instructions are so easy to follow, 10 year olds have websites. But if you run into a snag or you simply don't know how to proceed, call customer service. They will be happy to walk you through the process.

Social Media

If you know anything about online, you know that social media is the way to get it done. Build a Facebook Page and invite your friends. The difference between your profile and a page is that you can only have 5,000 friends on your profile. While that may work for now, you can have millions of followers on your page. That's how you grow. So, you should get started on that now.

A Facebook Page should have a dynamic header on it. You should keep your Facebook Page fresh with new content at least every day. Some of the bigger guys who are successful on Facebook have fresh content coming into their page several times a day.

Make sure your page is filled out with valuable information that lets users know who you are and what you are about. The most important things are that you have a site and you are selling your book. Interacting with groups and other high profile pages will help your page grow Likes. But remember, don't spam. Treat groups and pages like you want to be a valuable contribution and those people will check out your page.

You need to also build your Twitter following. Have the same header on Twitter that you do on your Facebook page. That's called branding. If you keep your message consistent, then branding will work out very well for you. Images of you should be consistent across all platforms. Background and header images should be resized to fit, but they should also be the same so that you look like you have a solid presentation.

You can keep fresh content on your Facebook and your Twitter by writing blog posts on your site. Interesting and entertaining posts that you can share to your Facebook page as well as to your Twitter. Your posts shouldn't always be about your book. But, there is a strategy to it.

First, what is your book about? Is there news that can direct attention to your book? What is going on in the world today that has any relevance to your book? When you start to look at news sources in that way, you begin to see how you can provide fresh content to your blog on a daily basis and share it around to all your social media profiles.

Facebook and Twitter were used as an example. But, you should also have a Linkedin profile as well as Goodreads. For a published author, Goodreads should not be overlooked. Pinterest, Instagram, and Youtube are also huge profiles that help people succeed online. Take pictures. Write articles. Make videos. Constantly post content on your profiles that are relevant to those sites and you will become a success.

To give you an example, you can make a quick Youtube video that has the potential to go viral. After you post it on Youtube, write something up about it on your blog. Share your blog post on Facebook and Twitter.

Take some still shots and post them on Instagram and Pinterest. Write up a gallery of photos on your blog. Share the blog post on Facebook and Twitter.

Keep your creative juices flowing. You can constantly come up with content that will keep your traffic flowing and your book sales skyrocketing. Just always be genuine and you will attract followers all day long.

Email Marketing

You can actually grow your list using your book. It depends on the purpose of your book. When you were thinking about it back when we discussed it, did you ever have any intentions of giving it away?

If you are a speaker or a consultant, those are two great careers where giving a book away can be very beneficial. Simply create an opt-in form that asks for names and emails. With a dynamic pitch, tell people to opt-in for their free copy of your book. Those names and emails will be very valuable to you as you have more to offer down the road.

Let your email list know about new products and speaking engagements. You can have them buying courses that you teach or future books that you write. A responsive email list is an extremely important resource that will be valuable to you as long as they keep reading your emails.

Of course, you don't have to give your book away in order to create an email list. Simply ask people to subscribe to your list. Put it in a prominent area of your site like on the sidebar to the right at the top. Some sites have popups with offers as soon as visitors land on the site.

Those offers can be about supplemental material that you may have. If you wrote a book about exercise, you could have supplemental material to give away like "7 Days to Better Abs." When visitors sign up on your list and get your document about better abs, you can send them updates and remind them about your book every time.

That's just one way to build your list with supplemental materials. You can offer a course that you implement in a series of emails. You don't have to teach the course. Simply send 9 or 12 emails that each teach a different lesson. That's your course. It's also a great way to build an email list.

Sit down and think of the many ways you can incorporate this idea. You might have to use some thinking to come up with something that hasn't been done before. But giving a book away for free or giving a course in a series of emails, they are strategies that have worked tremendously in the past. You might want to figure out how you can incorporate them into your campaign.

Joint Marketing Ventures

Go back through the notes you have when you were writing your book. Highlight every issue that came up in your book. Write down all the hobbies you may have mentioned. If you brought up any interests, talked about different occupations, and pretty much anything in your book that you can use to make a connection.

Then, make a spreadsheet. List all the issues, hobbies, interests, occupations, and everything else that you mentioned in your book. When you start to Google, list companies, organizations, and experts who you can connect with for a Joint Marketing Venture.

When you pitch them your idea, make sure you let them know how a Joint Marketing Venture can be beneficial to them. A pitch shouldn't be about how they can benefit you. That's not how you get their interest. But list all the ways in which the venture will put them in front of a new audience, give them a whole new platform, raise their revenues considerably, and what you bring to the table.

Of course, your book is a very strong point to pitch. With a solid marketing plan that you are putting together, you should have a pretty strong pitch for a Joint Marketing Venture. What you can do for them is most important. But, you also need to let them know their part.

Make sure that their contribution is equal to yours. If they are a strong partner to venture with, you might even want to do more. Just make sure what you are getting out of it has value. Most of the time it will.

Guerrilla Marketing and Joint Ventures by Jay Conrad Levinson and Sohail Khan is a great book to get ideas about putting joint ventures together. Of course, you have to approach each idea thinking as the author. You might be looking for an expert to do a joint venture with and suddenly realize because you have a book, you are the expert others are looking to venture with. Keep your value in mind and you can build great ventures that are going to help you out tremendously.

Writing Articles

Not only can you write articles on your site to keep your content fresh, but you can also offer articles to other sites. There are sites advertising for submissions. Help A Reporter or HARO is a great way to get into the news. But also, it's a great way to find out who needs articles written for them.

When you sign up to their list, they send emails out every day. You can sign up for as many lists as you want. Business, Finance, Fitness, and a plethora of other categories are available. It once was completely free and now still has the free basic package that sends you emails three times a day.

You can certainly get some valuable resources out of the free package. But, it doesn't hurt to look into packages that you have to pay per month. When you're talking about having your work highlighted on venues like *The New York Times*, *Time*, and *ABC*, it's worth looking into getting that kind of coverage. You could be the one writing the article and submitting it to a website for publication. You could also be the one getting a call from a journalist who is going to ask you some questions and your book magically appears in an article on a major online publication.

When you are on a site that has plenty of articles from different authors, get yourself into the habit of looking for their submission guidelines. They might even pay you for your work. Of course, you are getting a great benefit from having an author byline that mentions your book. But, getting paid isn't half bad either.

There is a strategy that you can employ that will make your search even easier. Google "write for us." Then, maneuver your cursor to the top right hand corner of the page and find the Options button. When you click on that, you will find Advanced Search listed. You can narrow your results to where the terms appear, whether they are in the title, in the text, or in links to the page. You can also narrow your search by last updated.

With all of the other features, these are pretty important. Keep your search relevant and up to date so that you can find sites that want your submissions and give clear submission guidelines for you to follow.

Guest Blogging is another way of providing articles on sites around the internet. Blogger Linkup and MyBlogGuest are the places to go to find out who needs articles for their blogs and how to get yours posted. Blogger Linkup allows you to browse for what owners of blogs need. You'll find plenty who are interested in topics that are relevant to your book.

MyBlogGuest is a forum where you can search through requests and find ones relevant to your book. There is a free version as well as paid versions. As with anything, start with the free version and see how that works. If you think you like the site and can do more with a paid version, by all means get in there and start writing articles. The more articles you have on the net, the more attention you are gaining for your book.

Podcasting

When you are looking into podcasting, there are two different ways to approach it. You can guest on podcasts if you are willing to do the research and find all the podcasts that would be lucky to have you. It's worth it to do the research and create a spreadsheet. Then, contact each one and give your pitch to get on their show.

The smaller ones will most likely have you on their show and their audiences are very interested listeners you can turn into book buyers if you can get comfortable and present yourself in an attractive way. It takes charisma if you have nothing to say.

It takes having something to say if you don't have charisma. A person with both is a shoe-in.

Some people though are actually looking into starting their own podcasts. If you have followers and think you can handle a show, then it's a way to go. It can actually lead into additional streams of income if your podcast becomes a success. You'll be able to sell advertising. You'll be able to have bigger personalities on your show. And your book will sell off the shelf like crazy.

Book Trailer

It's a little known strategy. But, a book trailer is a great way to sell books. Of course, it's a video that you can publish on Youtube and share to your social media. But, it doesn't have to be that difficult.

Some people have illustrations made for them that can be used as a slideshow. Find an artist on Fiverr.com and have them draw several screens. Read a script for 30 seconds and you have a decent book trailer. Using your imagination, you can come up with other great ideas to present your book to your viewers.

A book trailer could be contemporary news clippings that are relevant to your book. Cut them together and talk about how your book is relevant to the news of the day. With a 30 to 45 second video, you have a good trailer.

Sit down and write some ideas. Brainstorm about what kinds of ways can you visually represent your book. Then, look for the easiest way to make a video out of it. Don't make it harder than it has to be.

Paid Advertising

Google Adsense isn't the only online platform that places ads all over the internet. But, it is everywhere. Putting a Google Adsense campaign together is not a bad idea.

The thing about it is you can set your own budget. You can bid on clicks and set your budget so that the campaign stops when the amount of clicks has reached your budget. It's a safe way to do an online campaign that doesn't get out of hand.

You can write up an ad and do it the old school way. But, a banner for a headline or a sidebar are even better ways to get your message out there. People are very visual. If you give them a visual banner that has a great pitch and a call to action, you'll increase sales and that will justify having the Google Adsense campaign running.

In-Person Book Tour

When you're self-publishing, you have to act as your own manager. It can be challenging, but rewarding in the end. Some people even get a rush out of contacting people and setting everything up.

You can create your own book signing tour if you have the hustle to contact the right people. You can start with a local book tour where you visit local bookstores and cafes. Be creative! You don't always have to do a book signing in a bookstore. Coffee shops, libraries, malls, and other shops can all benefit from having an author come to their place of business and do a book signing.

Once you get the feel for it and you're comfortable, you can start setting up a book tour that takes you across several states. Contact radio stations and news channels in each area where you will be doing book signings. Try to have the shows before the day of the book signing so that you can pitch the event.

If a city you are in has talk shows, make sure you contact them too. Sometimes, they will be generous enough to buy a copy of your book for everyone in the audience. Then, you can talk about the book and let the viewers at home know about the book signing event.

It might take a lot of work. But, can you see how much success you can gain if you do it right? Don't let any opportunities slip through your fingers. Stay on your toes and look for any chance you have to push your book.

Online Book Tour

Online book tours aren't quite the same. You can set up podcasts and talk to their audiences about your book. But, you can also have different sites publishing reviews and posting blog posts that promote your book across the internet. It takes the same amount of hustle, but a different way of looking at things.

Some sites don't have enough ideas for content. They are perfect for promoting your book. You can actually write the content for them and have them publish it. It makes the whole process easier for them and you get in front of their users.

Online marketing has to be an ongoing task that you get yourself in the habit of doing and thinking about nonstop. There are always going to be opportunities that you are going to want to take advantage of when you see them. Jump on them. Don't let them slide by. That's when a successful online campaign starts to drop off and fade.

If you start writing a new book, don't stop promotion on your latest book. In fact, that's the best time to keep up promotions. You can include that you are writing a new book and when it will be out. You can already have the buzz going about the book you're writing if you never stop promoting the one you have out now.

CHAPTER 8

Summary

Publishing a book seems daunting at first, especially when you look at all the steps that go into make it happen. Some people are also disillusioned into thinking that once it's published, the work is done. Little do they know that it is just beginning.

It's just like anything else. Getting a product to the assembly line takes a lot of pain and hard work. But, that's just the beginning. The product has to be promoted before it has any reason to go out the door.

The same holds true with a book. You can put a lot of sweat and tears into writing it. You can rewrite ten to fifteen times to make sure that it's the best book you could ever present to anyone in the history of writing. But, it won't sell itself. Getting it published is the beginning of a long journey that can be both exciting and rewarding if you take the time to do it right.

When you write a book, you should know your purpose. It doesn't matter what the purpose is as long as you are honest with yourself. If you are only trying to write a book to make money, at least you are honest about it and every step you take can be properly planned so that you make the most out of it.

Some authors want to inform readers and make them aware of issues. Some authors want to tell a story and entertain their audience. Gurus can build a platform and establish themselves as experts in their fields. These are all perfectly legitimate reasons to write a book.

But, they dictate how you are going to write it and how you are going to promote it. Those details change from book to book. Some methods are generalized that cover any type of book you can write. But, other methods are only for specific types of books.

You make the whole process easier when you identify your exact purpose. That way you can plan from the beginning and you won't miss any steps.

For instance, a crime-solving drama can be written and rewritten to make sure the story is strong. Galleys can get sent off to the top book review sites on the net. A book tour can be setup along with radio spots and talk shows. A book signing tour can go from city to city for about three months if the author has the stamina.

But, a book about starting an online business can be given away to your website visitors so that you can build your email list. It's a totally different strategy because it's a totally different type of book.

When you sit down at the beginning of this project and map it all out, you streamline the process. You can go from start to finish in no time flat and have a very effective campaign up and running because you didn't waste time on steps that you didn't have to take.

Why would you send your short overview of starting an online business to the *New York Times* for a book review? You wouldn't. That step would be taken out of the game plan.

Of course, that was an obvious example. But, that is the point. When you know the purpose of your book and what you intend to accomplish with it, the game plan comes really easy.

Then all you have to do is make sure you write it. You can hire a writer to do that or you can give it a shot yourself. Remember, there are great editors out there you can hire to make sure your book makes sense and is error free. So, why not try writing your book yourself?

If you have the money, pay some to write it for you. You can actually have the entire process outsourced. You can have someone write it for you. You can have someone edit for you. You can have a team market it for you and set everything up that you need in order to make your online campaign a success.

If you have the money and you're not a good writer, that's the way to go. Your book is valuable to the potential readers who are waiting on it to be published. Outsource the entire process and get a great product in their hands.

It's one thing to say you're a carpenter and then hire out an entire team to build houses for you. It's a whole different thing to want to get your message out to readers and have a whole team work on the project with you. Those are still your words and they are important to your readers. That's why there is an entire industry built around getting books written, edited, and published.

Writing a book can be very rewarding. Whether you want monetary value out of it or just the intrinsic reward of knowing you actually did it, there's reward in it. It is addictive though.

If you follow through with everything in this book and you reach success with your first book, you'll definitely want to give it another try. You won't be able to walk away from an endeavor like this and not look back. That's why bestselling authors have a whole slew of books on their shelves.

Once you have written your first book, you realize it's not as hard as you once thought. Then, the ideas will keep rolling. Hope you have fun when you're writing and promoting your book. You can certainly make a difference in a lot of people's lives, as well as your own.

Afterword

Congratulations on finishing this book and taking the first step toward being a published author. We love helping people share their story and want to help you share yours.

Scriptor Publishing Group was created to make your dream of becoming a published author come true. If you are interested in getting more information about our services, please visit our website at www.ScriptorPublishingGroup.com.

In addition to working with authors through Scriptor Publishing Group, we also enjoy authoring our own books. Here are some of our books:

- **Greg Justice**
    - Treadside Manner: Confessions of a Serial Personal Trainer
    - Lies & Myths about Corporate Wellness

* Mind Your Own Fitness
* Mind Over Fatter: The Psychology of Weight Loss
* Mind Over Head Chatter: The Psychology of Athletic Success
* Mindset Over Matter
* Where FIT Happens: A Revolutionary Approach to Fitness
* Before You Swing: A Golfer's Guide to Fitness Training

- **Kelli O'Brien Corasanti**

  * Kelli's Quips: Happy Thoughts for Busy People
  * Finding My Way Back to Me: A Journey of Self-Discovery

We sincerely hope you enjoyed this book and want to thank you for taking the time to read it. Hopefully we've sparked a fire that will continue to burn.

To Your Success,

- Greg Justice & Kelli O'Brien Corasanti

About the Authors

Kelli O'Brien Corasanti is a co-founder of Scriptor Publishing Group and owner of Studio 8 Fitness, Inc. – a personal training and life transformation studio located in New Hartford, New York. She holds a Master's Degree in Counseling Education and certifications in Personal Training and Youth Fitness. She is the author of *Kelli's Quips: Happy Thoughts for Busy People* and *Finding My Way Back to Me: a Journey of Self-Discovery*. She is a Platinum Level coach for the Todd Durkin Mastermind Group and coaches fitness professionals around the world. Kelli is the recipient of the Accent on Excellence Award for her work throughout the community and was honored to be a presenter for the first TedX Utica program in 2013. For more information, go to www.sutdio8fitness.com

Greg Justice is a co-founder of Scriptor Publishing Group and owner of AYC Health & Fitness – Kansas City's Original Personal Training Studio, est. 1986. He holds a Master's Degree in HPER (Exercise Science) and was awarded Level II Master Trainer status by the National Fitness Hall of Fame. He has been actively involved in the fitness industry for more than three decades as a trainer, club manager, corporate wellness supervisor, and gym owner. He has authored 13 books including his signature book, *Treadside Manner: Confessions of a Serial Personal Trainer*. He also contributes to many international publications including, Men's Fitness, Women's Health, Prevention, Time, US New & World Report, and The New York Times. For more information, go to www.GregJustice.com or www.aycfit.com.

Author University Workbook

Define The Purpose of Your Book

(Use the next two pages to clearly define your books purpose)

_____

_____

_____

_____

_____

_____

_____

_____

_____

_____

_____

_____

_____

_____

_____

_____

_____

_____

_____

_____

_____

Create Your Mind Map

(Use these next two pages to do a brain dump for your book)

_____

_____

_____

_____

_____

_____

_____

_____

_____

_____

_____

_____

_____

_____

_____

_____

_____

_____

_____

_____

_____

_____

_____

_____

_____

Create Your Outline

(Use the next two pages to organize your mind map into an outline)

_____

_____

_____

_____

_____

_____

_____

_____

_____

_____

_____

_____

_____

_____

_____

_____

_____

_____

_____

_____

_____

_____

_____

_____

_____

_____

_____

_____

_____

_____

_____

_____

_____

_____

_____

_____

_____

_____

_____

_____

_____

_____

_____

_____

_____

_____

_____

_____

_____

_____

_____

Write Your Book

(Use the next two pages to practice writing your book)

Edit Your Book

(Use the next two pages to take notes while finding your editor)

_____

_____

_____

_____

_____

_____

_____

_____

_____

_____

_____

_____

_____

_____

_____

_____

_____

_____

_____

_____

_____

_____

_____

_____

Self-Publishing

(Use the next three pages to keep track of the step–by–step process of self-publishing)

_____

_____

_____

_____

_____

_____

_____

_____

_____

_____

_____

_____

_____

_____

_____

_____

_____

_____

_____

_____

_____

_____

_____

_____

Market Your Book

(Use the next three pages to take notes and develop a marketing strategy)

_____

_____

_____

_____

_____

_____

_____

_____

_____

_____

_____

_____

_____

_____

_____

_____

_____

_____

_____

_____

_____

_____

_____

_____

_____

_____

_____

_____

_____

_____

_____

_____

_____

_____

_____

_____

_____

_____

_____

_____

_____

_____

_____

_____

_____

_____

_____

_____